Mystic Orchards

Mystic Orchards

Poems by

Jonathan Koven

© 2023 Jonathan Koven. All rights reserved.
This material may not be reproduced in any form, published,
reprinted, recorded, performed, broadcast,
rewritten or redistributed without
the explicit permission of Jonathan Koven.
All such actions are strictly prohibited by law.

Cover image by Hedieh Ilchi
Cover design by Shay Culligan
Author photo by Audrey Gallagher

ISBN: 978-1-63980-425-2

Kelsay Books
502 South 1040 East, A-119
American Fork, Utah 84003
Kelsaybooks.com

For Delana,
my stillness,
my momentum,
universe all your own

Acknowledgments

Thank you to the following publications, which published early versions of some of the poems in this collection. Nearly all these poems have changed from their first appearances.

Cathexis Northwest: "Stethoscope"
The Dewdrop: "Stilled Wings"
The Dillydoun Review: "Future Is Older Than the Past"
Goat's Milk Magazine: "To Bring a Pulse," "Reason on the Horizon"
Lindenwood Review: "Long-sight"
Paragon Press' Echo: "Peppercorn and Backseat Windows," "Burgundy Responsibility"
Something or Other Publishing: "The White Wolf Dreams"

"Man Is the Intelligence of His Soil" is titled after Wallace Stevens' "The Comedian as the Letter C." "Oftentimes the Still Sad Music" is titled after William Wordsworth's "Lines Composed a Few Miles above Tintern Alley." "Future Is Older than the Past" is titled after a How to Dress Well song. "Waiting Makes Me Curious" is titled after a Fear Before the March of Flames song.

Endless gratitude to those who read earlier versions of this manuscript, and shared invaluable insights during the process. I give my dearest thanks and attribute this book's existence to the following: Bradley Galimore, Luna Rey Hall, Adam Gianforcaro, Sean Hanrahan, Yvonne Lee, Valerie Little, Samuel Fischer, Alison Lubar, Joseph Fasano, Beth Gordon, L.M. Camiolo, and many more wonderful talents . . . to Animal Heart Press for selecting an earlier draft as second-place runner-up for the 2022 AHP Prize . . . to Kelsay Books for publishing *Mystic Orchards* and allowing this collection to be widely read . . . to Hedieh Ilchi for granting me her sublime and transportive artwork . . . to my readers who I dearly cherish; thank you for allowing me this space and thank you for giving it your time and attention; I pray you find meaning in these pages.

Contents

1 SPIRIT OF GROWTH

Stilled Wings	19
Future Is Older Than the Past	20
Peppercorn and Backseat Windows	22
Dissolution Dream on the Verge of Bliss	24
Microscopic Pilots Fly Planes of Dust	25
After Light's End	26

2 A DARK HORIZON

Our Talisman	34
Stethoscope	35
Oftentimes the Still Sad Music	36
Ineffable	37
Waiting Makes Me Curious	38
Burgundy Responsibility	39
To Feed or To Nourish	40
Ambrosia	41
Everything Given	43

3 SYLVAN MEMORY

The White Wolf Dreams	47
I Read a Name in the Sun	51
For the Child in Love	53
Train Tickets to Swamp Bottom	54
Will You Breathe the Last of It?	55
As Birds Travel Far and Forever	57
Reason on the Horizon	59
The Canyon's Sapling	61

4 DEEPEST BLUE

Fingers Against the Window	65
Years Between	66
I Preserve You	68
Writing on the Wall	77
Insomnia Wish	78
Unburied	79

5 AWOKEN IN A FIELD OF LIGHT

My Dad Laughs	83
They Chirp About Destiny	84
In My City	85
Man Is the Intelligence of His Soil	86
Note on Time	88
Final Friend	89
Long-Sight	90
Eyes the Color of Inside the Earth	91
Cave Paint and Storm Songs	92
To Bring a Pulse	95

"If everything's just a dream
then let's dream, my soul
let's dream of happiness
because we know it will soon be grief."

—Pedro Calderón de la Barca, *Life is a Dream*
(t. by John Clifford)

1

SPIRIT OF GROWTH

"And never far away is the lightning of the heart that quickens the need to understand the night sky as a word . . ."

—Joy Harjo, "Petroglyph"

///

Daze saves from the daze. The mind banners in the dark, when no wind blows, when no one watches.

(I love you in the cricket swell, in the acid snowfall, I love you in the crank of machines, in the shattered glass of bedroom windows one million years in the future, I love you in the new jungle, reborn again and again)

Somehow, from elsewhere, we arrived here, how you too felt part of nature, in the summertime, barely a teen, bare feet in the shallow, looking far as you can see, to know the world waits and happens in the waiting. I was the water around your ankles, running, running again to the farthest knoll—

Stilled Wings

Past the farthest knoll I drag
sacks of dead fireflies
No longer do their strobes glow

Toss fistfuls into a wishing well
Watch sound-circles
remember glimmering tails

In the cold black water
moonlight envisions gardens
their stilled wings will soar

Future Is Older Than the Past

Something blooms—
for all I see, in smoke
and shadow, weaves
universes all their own.

Out of a dream within dream,
cyclopean surgeons whisper
to peel clouds
like petals from sky,

I love you, I love you not, until only blue.
In wake, unfurl as a poem
no one reads, its metaphors
mixing in the end;

and drain the moon its silver,
and wilt its daffodils,
only to water them to new life,
and beauty beyond death.

Here, I stand still
with hopeless descent of the mind,
to compose my inner child, he who considers
imagined future, older than anything at all,

while hearts rend to recapture
subterranean as constellation, to paint a lake
to drown my sorrows, and maybe someone else's.
Not everyone will know what I hope I know.

Nothing is sordid about this scream.
Glory's serenade outside heaven's gate:
*You am there
and I are here.*

To believe this rips out our roots
to before the dream began;
to finally see the light
at the end of light's end;

I have circled longer
than Jovian rings measure, watching
the brimstone and plasma, blooming
universes on my own.

Peppercorn and Backseat Windows

It is that veiled time.
Elms amber,
take down, and
pale.

Sweet teeth fill mouths,
car-seat quiet, carving
I and *love*
and *you*.

So far ago, it is again.
We wear November, count days
the brume lowers within.
Coat drip, a yester breeze,
a whiskey sky; roaming
a still life.

Your hands are cold. Remember,
I was a boy whose beltways listened,
whose irises willowed
to catch rain.
A wish to keep away the cold.

A wrist
against window, a palm
under my head; I sink
beneath eyes' brine to hieroglyphs
and white flags waving.
Phantom sails.

Tonight might become beautiful.
I delicate after beautiful pain.
And that peppercorn swiftly
askew pensive hearts: now,
until I die. For us,
and every other reverie

on repeat.

Dissolution Dream on the Verge of Bliss

Should I meet the sky-mantis,
I'll ask to be cradled in the milk of stars,
brown eyes burnt honey,
gliding on high silence.

My spirit will clatter its cage,
out wind-plucked chambers cascades
pumpless silver sleeves
homeward the crashing ocean.

I see her there in a blaze of wisdom.
Coax the shame from my sleep.
Lend me language again, any at all,
to embrace a new god on the unreal plane.

Breath is a hero;
color, a container;
forest, the dreamer.

I'll run, run, run
to forever
remember you.

Microscopic Pilots Fly Planes of Dust

Black river spills over

Earth

Dear God who knows no name
The mind frolics
Pumped by its need
To the mystic orchards

What the speedy call dying
Means living

My sorrow is older
Than any shape it takes
But even the sky moves

To silence
My soul

To cede the black river
Seek destiny as dust

My childhood battles
Society and solitude within
A heart painted green
Metronomes the rapids

The black river gushes

Speech
Nourishing the myth
As rain freezes to snow

Then diaspora
No one listens at all

Where whispers undress
Colder
Chatters like charring oak
Underneath
A ravenous tongue
Lashes

Guides away

After Light's End

Blue moon coins voltage
to sever the unholy sky.
World, a sole heart, the meat colossus.

Lightning courses striae, tours arterial.
And rain softens Earth with pelting cherubim.

Surviving,
surviving,
surviving enough.

Remember me from sea's surface.
You promised something else above.

///

Oaken boughs twine in frame of a doe
foaming from wolf's bite—
a helpless perpetrator—purpling,
purpling dead leaves, too.

The doe groans, abandons her snare
of boughs to cliff's edge. A pause,
trip, and fall, stolen by the water.

The undrinkable brooms; poison
wildflower as harbor falls off
with her—covering the gentle child
from rain—coalesces. And away . . .

///

In a ring of yellow spotted bamboo. The weather keeps. Deaths like this hail by the hour. Notating to stay sane . . .

. . . watched a deer nearby—venison no good—sad thing seemed sick. It rested a long while, likely to hold off pain. Nearly fell asleep myself watching. Then, branches buffeted; a whimpering. Between red leaves its darting eyes. Little thing whinnied, thrashed, cut through vines and poison oak, until the cliff ended too soon to notice. Tumbled into the canal. Shimmered away useless hunger for the mind.

I wonder: does a will to live empower at the end? My exhaustion bests my starvation.

Been watching these scarlet waters. I notice patterns, like a spirit might sleep below topsoil; chest rising, falling. The waves hypnotize, daring to drink. But it is full of sick.

To live this long, to see what we have done before we all die.

I try to remember years ago: springs after winters, out of loneliness the onset of warmth. Seeking faces among others. Friends, on streets, anywhere. To find who would catch us, one who stays. Quick, the cities burned, the water poisoned.

Before this was a time when humans did not exist. Maybe, after the last fires, after the animals eat each other, after the poison filters clean, I'll be dead. And out of my body, new creatures will fly.

///

Soon, never
a deer again.

Within patient oak arms,
I await my turn. I die
in this world, whose sky sags
red flesh over the country.

I still honor you
despite all things dead, taken by the canal,
having waited to understand charm in the sorrow
of waiting, hope among it all, after the humans
poisoned us, and primal starlight returned.

Off in the distance, I spy a human among
the yellow-spotted bamboo. He may
very well be the last. I honor all of you
who died to give breath to this man.
He will be gone soon, anyhow.
I will be gone soon. The heat begins
in my hooves, white, deafening electricity
through thinned veins.
I might instead drink the green water.
Its splashing tells a secret
from so long ago.

///

Current carries
generations of children.
Prayer books. Tape reel.
Bottles. Bones.
Before cities were built,
and all that has awakened
after they have fallen.
Promises, lullabies,
millennium of moments, shared,
blended. I am
the canal. I am the here
and there. The doe
falls with me,
united by the water.
And we feel it together, a green spill into ears,
softly cresting ancient stars on marrow's rush.

With her
I hear
stories she receives
in sinking,
a clear message in the calm
of all things dead:
I love you, too.

I love
you, too.

2

A DARK HORIZON

"... and sometimes in the sunlight my eyes,
walled in water, would glimpse the pathway
to the great sea."

—Frank O'Hara, "River"

///

With care, my mother plucks pomegranate seeds. Some say we live one of two ways, facing shore or sea, and as she decides, slow the rove of a star's chamber for pearls, and sleepily shed rosiest gleam to whatever awaits.

Sometimes I am quiet in return; still, my mother knows my lows early as they arrive.

She remembers when the Andes Mountains leaned back for the morning dew, jacaranda rising, creeping wine stalks, slowing cattle, a blue sky yawning; the *somehow* and the *all-at-once;* first Paraguay, then Argentina, her hands learned stasis. Her voice brought kindness to Brooklyn streets. With wind at her back and words in her chest.

My mother, before dawn, writing reminders on baggie lunches; my mother, silent on island train tracks; in the evenings, giggling through the dim, pitting pomegranates.

I carry her sweetness to simmer in the lungs, sonnets of patience. Easily bruised but I know to survive because of her, to move, to mend hurt, to care about hurting anything else. To look out windows, to chase shore or sea.

Where she is, is where I'll be.

Our Talisman

I still cry through
My father's eyes

        Take my mother's path
        Fast to hold it lonely

We sages of dust
        Childhood a jewel

Trust we all vanish
        Without a trace

        Slow our hearts diffuse
To vespers ascending

Kindle stars awake
        Behind storm dark skies

        Contrails vein the clapping
Pulse of lightning

        Years to timid Earth
Turn us to prayer again

Stethoscope

I recalled origin's solace
before breathing, promised a chance
to see Buenos Aires of a past generation.

(My great uncle, the activist,
                was killed in captivity)

Some deadbolts twitched my mother's heart.
My preamble: a greaser of its jangle, guardian
of the endless sound inside.

No screams leaving the womb; I hummed
the theme to *Titanic,* proud to be American,
a harbinger of loss.

Meanwhile, bombs gurgled on television;
counting *Pokemon* cards while
the World Trade Center was destroyed.
Content, quiet for the Pledge; unseen,
untouched, under the haystack, fast asleep.

A twilit Montauk shore rejoiced
in my late remembrance of repression.
Once, there was great melody
in my waiting, and the waiting still sang.

I held the mainland in
all my chaos and wept, "Please,
don't hurt me again."

Oftentimes the Still Sad Music

The bell tolls. Mad clown's diatribe warps high
over the trackless nation, across the soot
sully, through gunpowder plume, home;
wrapped in a hideous blanket of ineloquence.

He purges boyish want shared by many—to fill
empyrean ears with a serpent's libel. They ask,
Why is heaven not already beneath their feet?

Defer to the turnstile registering ennui
to sadness more sublime: candles for teeth,
suburban cinemas over indigenous graves,
lovers' hands and not antennae mad for power,
thieving tomorrows, one after the next.

One can only hope, someday, silence will take
the shape of an old slow morning, when
homeless children awake with flushed eyes,
in cities where pale buildings purple
come evening, sapping sadness from the bark
of their being; asphalt overgrown,
softer to sleep upon, and ignore the promise
of a crimson balloon getting bigger.

Tracks rattle a world in the mind, carrying
worn travelers to where the nightingales chitter.
The chasm left behind brims with the hymn.
Red leaves swoop new order; every echo rewinds.

Ineffable

clouds eclipse
                                      colonize the plain
                                   I envy a simpler story
                                           in dark greens

each sunbeam on my soul
torments those cold in secret
but the details are as weeds
in concrete or as roots in topsoil
architectures of a deep truth   in and of itself

                    art and luxury masters of disguise
                I emblazon by the sun's ease of bliss

see there is a beautiful Earth inside me
to explain without the right words
reverse wastelands to chaparral
I think my thoughts scatter
in everyone I've yet to meet

I want them all to   look upon my forest
                              burning at the edges
                              the middle is golden

listen beneath the pond
there rests the nation's killed

withered   lungs relearned
                              their filter of the smoke
waiting for their truths   to be heard

Waiting Makes Me Curious (My Parents Compare Depression to Paralysis)

I'm driving my car at eleven. Stars, weather like crickets. Windows, tired eyelids. I'm driving my car at eleven. Slow waves comb in; further above, buckets pour over with sleepy lightning. Cool air as alarm, I'm driving my car at eleven, and I'm driving my car at eleven, and the moon is a buoy or a wound. Tedium ebbs, years away, years back into self.

And I'm driving my car at eleven, a number like twin roads. The moon floats, gores over crickets. Sacrificed to invisible platinum. Underneath, heart's fabric untangles, twangs a chance rhythm: *Moloch*. A wish without admitting my exile. It could be the first night—the only night—of my life: the expressway, and I'm driving my car at eleven. Radiant the rims of sudden laughter. And on the next night, I'm driving my car at eleven.

Maple leaves parch orange as the moon, crunch under tires. Will the cricket swell end? I'm secretly worried that the last summer loll ends with it, as easiness exits the flesh (it has, it will); goosebumps borne from the purge.

I'm driving my car at eleven, then I'm driving my car at eleven. *What if the road falls into the sky? . . . What if it has?* Even darkness steeps in waiting, believing waiting is like water. I breathe between where I'm from, where I'll go. I'm driving my car at eleven, to conquer both, to confront neither. I'm driving my car at eleven.

Burgundy Responsibility

Halted wristwatch atop
the night table, too soon
to resuscitate, whittles
braver futures
between

both seconds sealing where
a stagger in time starts,
and

>(she is a pilgrim of sugar; she is
now sprinting
inside the greenhouse;

>she is kneeling in fauna; she is
exhuming
blares of an alarm;

>she is unconquered time. I pine
for a stalling
of the smaller hand

where it drops.)

To Feed or To Nourish

we are an odd bunch,
stilted bodies, rotating
thinking we are trees under a red sun

before winter is over, we will grow apples
on our arms (again before winter)
we will be saplings in the baggiest clothes

remember the sharp pang of New Year's Eve,
only teenagers reeling our dumb stridence
until smithereens; us, opened to eclectic sky

I made the same wish; every Saturday weighed
our American weekends
and it made me stay (alive)

the echo was free; every Saturday slowed
our overdoses, fighting
the rot of year-old sky

blood on my teeth, I found a map
in a January memory
(for us, for only us) we are trees

under the red lawn, to wish
for firelight
and never disappear

Ambrosia

I hear the wolves
crooning in my mind, where glory reigns,
killing guiltlessly with friends.

How iridescent this carol, despite all
the bleeding, a garden
distanced from onrush,
below chatter of a bodied mountain,
the song rouses itself alive.

Today, tremble knowing this sacrament
belies meat, pulse, water, stone;
everything, a theory tested.
Incautious, as in phantasm, bison roam.

///

Spread me wide
with this brand of summer. Make rivers flow
out my mouth, a trembling bowstring of spine
to pull back,
hold tight, or else remember
a lullaby sung to me,
"Arrorró mi sol, arrorró pedazo
de mi corazón."
Each season quests peaceful sleep,
clasping my amnesia, and pray the song's promise,
"Duérmete mi nene, duérmete pedazo
de mi corazón."

///

Born fleck of star, dropped
into east Atlantic sea,
traveled by trout-mouth

through cicada shells
and cigarettes,

to pull cogs from clocks, words
from infancy,
banish classification of veins,

to regret my bedlam,
disguised an agent of chaos,
and fall away to love.

///

The harmony unites
millions of timbres
and to shout along
is to learn
of a basic creature inside.

Inside me,
a gallows swinger
plays to-and-fro;
yet, merely a happy child
amused with a rope.

Everything Given

I've been to many a home, translated
sonnets to patterns in drone,
sirens beckoning. I pull my weight
into the deep.

No eye behind vastness but a sky
in the eye. In a dream I wander inside
to fall asleep under the tallest yew,
fated to infinities.

In wake, I lift free from a tangle of roots
twined for the stasis of skeleton.
I want a pond to reel in the past,
but this is the scope of God.

A fire reads a verse that cleans cities to rubble,
a star erupts and manifests one destiny.
I hear a voice like mine. *You don't have to.*
I touch my flesh and remember I'm alive.

3

SYLVAN MEMORY

"Eternal rivers flow beneath the window of my silence.
I never stop seeing the far shore. . ."

—Fernando Pessoa, *The Book of Disquiet*
(t. by Richard Zenith)

The White Wolf Dreams

"And we are magic talking to itself,
noisy and alone."
   —Brigit Pegeen Kelly

Clouds vacuumed in quiet, shaving the plateau bone white. The skyline still held a maroon glint. Dawn. Surrounded by glacial mountains, the color was soft enough to miss. Yet, it leaked, coring in the frost a ring of the sun—where the White Wolf slept.

The White Wolf did dream, as animals do, of her children. When she awoke, their absence bore deeper. Paws tucked under her, she whimpered, though she was glad for the warm light.

A moan replied beyond the massive ice wall. She lifted like a breeze in its direction. *Was it them? Could it be them?* The horizon's sliver opened its gash, pouring not sunlight, but a reel of smolder; a singed, boiling haze. From its stain, wind rollicked the lowland, and The White Wolf's spine straightened. She felt summoned.

She limped to plateau's end, at the foot of the hill, and pawed at its icy path. She would not be able to climb without slipping. Cold snow huddled, and she cried again.

The moan answered, voice cracking like melting ice.

There was no way around. To discover the source of this sound, she must scale the mountain and see beyond the glacier's edge.

Hungry, she persisted. It had been days since the last meal. Since the blood-lights first razed the dead sky above, no pulse stirred on the plateau. Only the White Wolf and the wilted earth had watched the sun pass overhead. She remembered the nights of tectonic roaring, her paws sliding, slipping, leaping; her stomach grumbling passing the firepits, rich with the nutty fragrance of roasting meat;

and swimming—swimming in the cold sea, under the hot smoke—swimming under tides thrashing, between floating glass; she remembered escaping the clip and the shot, the blinding lights, the bone-crackle and splash. She remembered her children but forgot exactly where and when they separated. The details obscured as hunger grew.

When the White Wolf had escaped the fires and fighting, when she had finally reached the plateau, the roaring had finally settled. Yet, she had not expected the quiet to be worse. Exhausted from silence, like it was an unending ringing in her ears, she had needed sound: a burning desperate plea, a hark in black night—anything—to resound in that emptiness. And there had been a moan, perhaps a whimper or a cry. She could not waste this chance.

She howled. A howl came back.

Clawing up the icy hill, she saw a snowbank ahead. The White Wolf rammed her body against the ice, cold stinging her snout. Snow scattered, flourishing the air. She rejoiced, carefully climbing where the snow fell, certain not to slip on the wet slide beneath.

Hours later, she reached the summit's crest. She panted heavily, swallowing her own saliva for thirst.

The lights above danced like the swirling blood of civilization. They breathed, threading themselves between stars and milking off into grey mist. She felt her heels lift her into the flare, where no darkness—no shadow passed at all—sky a pool, a spinning phosphorescent void, draining sound.

She barked softly, weak. Nothing spoke back.

The White Wolf carefully slid down, then chased to the hill's foot, on the other side of the mountain. It looked the same, matted with snow, stretching for miles.

There! A silhouetted figure elevating from the blankness. It also lifted, pulled into celestial hands of spilling color.

The White Wolf rushed, barking. The reply, louder now, pierced her ears like a siren. She barked again. Something called back. *Was it them? Could it be them?* Like the whorl above, a storm teemed her skull; a sparkle behind her eyes flowered in darkness; a white firework spattered. She could not see anything, only the whiteness of snow and noise itself, coursing past her.

She arrived at the figure's edge. An abandoned boat, sail tattered upon the deck, was frozen in the snow. Splinters of wood littered the surrounding ground. Her long nails scratched the cold deck, feeling hollowness inside-and-out. The White Wolf whimpered.

The boat whimpered back, slower.

She had only heard her echo. There was nobody and nothing on this frozen boat, merely the memory of a certain motivation—to go somewhere, to arrive elsewhere. Without a creak, it voicelessly prayed its voyage on the deadest ocean, rocking a hull against imagined waves. Pinned down, it only existed a silhouette; to be appreciated from afar, to hear the echo of one's last chant, to be realized as distilled adventure—bearing nothing but empty promise.

Yet her echoes, when the White Wolf heard them, boomed glorious pain of surviving. It proved something, despite she the only who listened.

She lay on the tattered sail, cradling her own body in the warmth of dreams.

The sky's dancing sleeves continued burning. And the silence resumed.

I Read a Name in the Sun

hear a parable I once trusted
of wish maker gone
to the water   a wanderer turned
water strider

through timeless gullies
those august glints ever dashing

high with gnats   loud on peaches
sexing under crackling suppressed sky

relapses to summer psychedelia
to spite the very choice
in daily resurrection

but that stupid story
tells itself anyway

a dead friend once spoke the moral
immediately forgotten
my eyesight: misremembrance

instead   I choose you
kiss me in the afternoons
my stormy eyes still see

old heart many chambered
aroar in final fortune
antennae tangled   to voyage
as when you were young

as for the next legend to live by
it could be one word

love continues   to reveal
simpler purer dialect
we all deserve this beautiful drift

For the Child in Love

Dearest reader,
sky's a stolid blue until sight enters
like a swig to a swallow.
For you, for what is plain
calcifies color;
for you, who steers transparent tongue
toward sunray in song (jaybird crossing
the brain); you, who falls
to symbols, we mission to escape the real.
This is for whoever cores the poison apple, reeling
seeds for a newborn forest, and for whoever waits
to clench, at those aged canopies,
God in the mist at dawn—poetry
a channel to gratitude, or a strange blue veil over death;
for you, follower of raindrops
to window corners, seeing in them a memory; sunlight,
laughter; earth,
body; I know
everyone keeps a story to share, and another
to repeat to oneself; their sentences run long,
twin confessions in realization of agreement,
to feel free once; as in all hearts
an image of the freest self,
forever a child in love. Ordering all chaos,
beauty summons my sense that to receive
this letter means I was never mine; now
yours, everlasting.

Train Tickets to Swamp Bottom

See, the sky rinses this village, us
babbling spirits, those bananas
on branches. Careful what mortals call fugue!
We mind no *fix* to those bewitched
quickly, like water fills
sinkholes with mirrors of constellations.
When happiness arrives at
a station, funnels spin in sundry drains; watch
our hands turn gold by your celebration.
Our children click tongues and
play with yellow peels.

If you wish to find her, there are tracks ways out
from here: follow your fever at dusk, pour
over the cliffside into
earthen gutters come moonrise, to
the last thing admitted—we lonely,
we lonely few conjure completely,
like reliving a childhood fantasy.
But watch the clouds herd shapes
in framing of your love's face. It is all
the same to know
to follow the last road home.

Will You Breathe the Last of It?

Baby born
Ruminator
Blossom on the water

Grow curious
For starless knowledge
Nonbinary beauty or pain

Curate tasteless pixels
Whet your lungs with fancy
Breathe the last of it

Death drafts windows
Laminates years
Memories

Behold timeless dataflow
Strident reefs
Arcs sempiternal shadow

The vast mantle unhooks
Observe your face
On the other side of a screen

Avatars simulate
Adjust and recalibrate
Fragments of a spirit

Rain collects on trash bin tops
No one to blame
No fawning for attention

Understand this code
Before inhabiting a body
A secret unremembered

And yet
A needless urge of the heart
Always felt

To draw maps of light
As it reaches this rock
To borrow one chance

While cinders spore dawn's flame
Smattering new Saturn
In the palm of its eclipse

As Birds Travel Far and Forever

Shallow praise despite smiles' might.
Everything   never enough.

The sculptor resigns before madness,
chaser of infinite pursuit. Watches
a gouge in night's rubied flesh, blackbird
blued in glow, carve the lunar well to leaks.

Wants to name   God,
wants to be part   of the many parts of God.

Weather's force to allow
tomorrow, greeting wonder
as a shapeless being.

Shards fall from greater wonderment.
First, considers memory but knows
told tales depart wind-coo, less than
dust after end days, comforts
in arrangement of miracles,
mementos, reconciliations.

These encounters derive manna through
a shared primordial soul, like chirps sounding
out framework, never meant to transpose.

And so, it ends
to let begin,

listening for form
listening for release
transfixed   in flight   forever

Violet at zenith, grace notes fray the
sacred wretched exhalation. But learning
by passing into humdrum, to seek no lands,
no divine stone
beyond clay—

true artists aspire such simplicity. Naked,
mute confession slipstreams,
exalted lifetime mire but unfinished.

Notion glorifies a break:
a blackbird chronicling softly.
Listening for the quiet—

but a bird,　　　　　absent without clay.
Nothing else　　　　is enough.

Reason on the Horizon

    walls   croon

    wild   heart

    smoke   batters

          unapologetic

          (*spirit blade*)

    glimmer   dance

          bedspread

    glass   torching

          (*fire afire*)

    ever   hopeful

          enchantress

    melody   raveling

          (*night gossamer*)

I see you there

magenta   thrill

bids   farewell

(*iceblink siren*)

high   pines

never   ending

phone   wires

everlasting

(*in one ear   out forever*)

I hear you there

The Canyon's Sapling

She paints this sapling,
lichen prince stranded at precipice.
Alights leafless limbs, calligraphic
over swing set belly.
January whistles between tree's fingers
splaying out crags.
Hope waits atop the tallest peak,
teachers have said,
rain flowing out their mouths,
chiseling thirsty crevices behind eyes,
should wandering tire her to their hollows,
never to admit respite.

This sapling symbolizes
her hope, but the canyon hinders discovery.
A starving vulture preys the expanse.
Does it care what's lost in scalp's blush,
what sadness ensures hungrier scour?
No one climbs or falls in a virtual world.
The painter eclipses the canyon with clouds,
masts one sun glint
for the deviant enamored with hope,
endowing presumed fate: slow death
to the death eater. Life remains
in the still image.

4

DEEPEST BLUE

"Musical madness keeps me from sadness,
I'll just keep playing guitar.
I keep, keep on strumming
forever, I'm yours till the end of time."

—My dad, Neil Koven, "Musical Madness"

Fingers Against the Window

I wait three hundred years in this house with nothing but fate in my hands. To see him; under the covers, a boy who melts, who washes over planet's edge. He sleeps, he spills, he comes together again when my eyes are closed.

Whitewash heaves, ghosts tuning their guitars. For three hundred years, wind beyond the walls. A terracotta murk mantles the Pleiades, blush of a bruised peach, and planes gash pulp to betray pit.

If I knew anything else, I would write it. To offer breath to bramble. To rise my lips to summer snow, rend my networks of every nerve. I am in my room and the world is happening. I should say it to myself. *The world happens, the world is happening.*

Terracotta, morning of bated breath, you are my cold delirium. Now, it is too late. I cannot save you.

When three hundred years are over, I drop my fate into piles of laundry and walk out the door. I become the puddle I was destined to be. Patient, sleepless, perfect mirror of sky.

Watch me ripple if you dip a finger. Pour me into your ears. It is the sound of running too fast. A part of you also believes in lifting away, into the terracotta, if you would just let go.

Years Between

The wind blew through
my ribcage's bookshelves,
swam through its spaces,
novels tumbling, slid out
under my lungs, collected
heavy at my feet, to drag,
to drop.

I still find their words, trampled,
portals upon pavement.
Quotes I had assumed forgotten,
geological tribute,
artifice of miracles,

outside
bonded
inside,
fragments left
for a new self.

Walking home to greatest happiness,
reading archetypes, decades since,
I see "keep," and "waiting," and "onward."
Words so defining, somehow vanished.

All the while, the sky windows a view
of a childlike stranger
wearing a terrific mask of my aged face.

The stranger's limbs lift, flex
stretchmarks spanning clouds.
Ripples. Conjure a poem from
a vague ambition I followed
without assurance, yet it led
to this moment, remembering
the time until—

blood of eternity
fills all
my empty spaces.

What does memory make
of depression born in fiction?
I, its writer
and reader.

Someday, I will learn
youth is a story,
not red in veins.

Future, fantasy.
Here I am.
Here I am.

I Preserve You

Born to a mosquito dream
waiting for God
to sip my skin clean of August
to spike my cells

Lost blissful unaware
in dewy pipeline of critter psalm
below branches sun-blued
and enraptured by the words:

And Yet
Some giant spoke them

Delusion my blue seed
but is my God
a memory of a feeling never felt
never to feel again?

And Yet
refrain reminds

*I'll wait to see you
in whatever's after life*

///

She wakes, turns toward windows, watches
wind sleeve jacaranda, hands of purple fortune
forfeit God's first confession: forgiveness
neighbors remembrance
as sea dashes sand
      Every melting,
       every pearling
(every dream we dream alone,
despite poetics or deepest breaths,
though passion gapes for starlings to read)
alive in a story retold, misunderstanding
its impossible truth:

every sound cacophonies,
      every breathing beats the dead,
      every vision twirls mystery,
garment, reverie, or worse

No protection survives her arrival
at the idea of being
one century,
one reverberation,
one yesterday or tomorrow spent thinking
of yesterday and tomorrow

      Like her, I keep the same pulse:
an old way sung before
      and what's left to see

God, why must the instant blue so soon
(everywhen blues), kindling ancient want
to become a trillion eons
in scatter? as if life renews
beyond the grave

And Yet how simple is a push
followed by a pull,
if pattern steals everything?

O sunray
sunray, sunray, rainfall,
moon bloom;
everyone, listening
for gospel in longing, light
swollen in ligaments
drawn to the flame,
sent to the edge again,
breathing deep only after
remembering that we die

(*And Yet* every dream we dream
alone, of footsteps untaken,
a bridge to gratitude or another bridge;
even still, I revere despair's force
to clearing space
for deepened dream
to seal out the catch,   everything
as it might be and might not be,
in the clarity   of daylight)

///

My father, eternal Canarsie kid, subscribed
to highways, stealthy by summer,
disbelieved childhood's end
I'll wait to see you
in whatever's after life—
chorused a godawful source,

pill after pill
to pursue abyssal purple,
to reenter scorned fantasy,
to keep love safe, in that   love
meant safety, that love could keep safe
and conquer truth   but never so

Outward from the source,
everywhen he roams   learning
of his mother's heart, before,
an old way danced   to *Rhapsody in Blue*
and songs her own mother loved,
all for past's soft despair;
a film I watch later
in hallucinogen pyre, District drone-pipe,
wondering where the forgotten goes
despite fossilization
of my sheltered youth, happiness
in spite of it—but is my happiness true?

All the while, inward from the source,
forgiveness—who else would forgive us
if not strangers in other cars we share
glances with, deciding against a risk
to cross and destroy us both? remembering
every friend who forgot, every dropped
dream, vaulting his years   on years
for new names,
lifetimes reconciled,
praying for me to be, to *be*   and I was
his son and I am his son and forever a son,
a stranger in another car, a friend who forgets

My mind roars, too, *I'll wait to see you in
whatever's after life,* like the Canarsie kid,
the newfound childhood woken into
after his long high; like children who die
or whose childhoods warp to dreams,
even those draining eyes of dreams,
begging future to appear, baiting freedom
to wait   for the answer
to an unanswerable question, for another
apology for my salvation, for forgetting
while knowing nobody remembers; and
because of this   I forgive us all

My mother also dreamed
like the mosquito, an Argentine teenager
arriving with my grandmother to America,
a garden promised over graveyards;

instead, cemented braveries
of their own, knowing it was hard
being here at all   at the verge
of new mythos, unraveling a facade
of refuge to ire   attuned
like mosquitos, alive with undying intention,
as fate heeds the unspoken cry for more;
meanwhile, we all wait for everywhen

My own survival a drug, I laugh
at this performance, feigning
time's defeat, driven songward
by fear, obviously lost
to years between, always years
between now and being

a stunted boy listening to trees, devoured
by unshakable fear   of loss,
aging   misremembering,
not feeling I met the moment,
and still somehow seeming
most important are the years between

In them, I forget
my father's purple abyss and
I forget my brother's silenced fear and
I forget my mother's waiting, resisting,
quiet as evening's draft, another and
another   until buried;

I forget how I forget so I remember to live
like a child in love, unbound
to hometown's dead ends   gilded
by purest survival unless seen
senseless, numb to how it blues,
whispering, *I'll wait to see you in heaven*

you (and you, and you . . .) remind me of
softness in thunder, cozied
through God's mouth or universal soul,
again into blue, into the mirror
we become, of a century in wonder,
kindness prevailing   through
reduced reality; though, milliseconds ago,
my mother praised my first poem
(my second, my third), realizing an answer
to who I may eventually become,
insoluble because
we always become   like one another

And Yet of private imagining
backyard scenes with Andrew, beholden
to brotherly inventions,
pouring over invented blue,
below tides, time brining us
dreamers in seismic brash, treading
to our own music   realizing
the present was—is God,
all along on spellbound suburban streets;
afterlife a headache   amen
to a waking dream, reconciling regret,
living through loss

Now here, a fragment of infinity,
I am already forgetting
this moment among the newest frolic,
the oldest ocean's vow, a song
for century's end,
coursing veins
this confession   I love you
as I forget the lesser details, replacing
with blueness   expanding greater
than any reality, though none might fix
such joyous shade to memory
of a feeling never felt, never to feel again

///

God, if you want a prayer, my words are yours
until I have none left or I burst with them,
cascading as fractals or equations
launching from blankness,
then my family could sense sky's ridges,

build schemes with them, or else fall
gently into each other's arms   maybe I learn
my pain was always free, gifted
by myself for myself, though I transcribe it
to feel you

I believe I remember you, too,
despite years between,
in shields of dust   by stars
or disease where I grew this tremendous
yearning of the heart

And Yet   *And Yet*   *And Yet*

Writing on the Wall

When you were young, your soul was saltwater on forearms. Inky wrists. Scabbed knees. You forgot how your father shut his door, how your mother opened hers. Each cloud peppered with sunlight. Secret years swayed into sea wind. You believed, heaven is a fast car flooded in music, an exposed spine, dry heaving, a goodbye said tomorrow afternoon. Love slipped over suburbia—arguments of bored siblings, first wanderlust, pale rooves juggling stars, bulbs chirring like rain. Summers passed easy and, below your bedroom carpet, your parents' whispers, loosening their tourniquets too tight. Gazed at the ceiling washing ashore your canvas, listening carefully to tremors in arrested white, a heart's thrum became voice's muted falsetto. How you ran into the backyard. The surface of the sky flexed, stars velveting. *Don't let the island crawl over you. But don't let it swim away.* Impossible wish. That was when you waited for your father's long night to pass, when you watched your mother watch him. Those childhood bedroom walls wrote themselves a message, something learned after leaving; trust feels less like other people, more a shelter, or maybe sunlit waters lifting mirage. Nicked ankles with tree bark, climbing to catch dappling, your soul swallowed sky to digest under dredges of love. How to best utter your wish. When to give away your fear. Remind yourself not to forget: don't hurt until it is done. The heavy weights sold strength, to keep your lonely wonder. When love scoured the sky, you watched it take everything everywhere. It went wherever light painted pavements below.

Insomnia Wish

sleeper in my brain   I will find you to know you
on the last turnpike   when blue stars freeze over
rock rose overgrown   and a singing in the clouds

before morning's alabaster breaks city shoulders
and night's silver dewed panther
slips under the polluted moon

when primal desire from the lonely
seeps dreams or drunk darkness
after mist has fallen to rinse every record of home

let me awaken you   from ever-expanding sleep
while harmony dawns   softness to old apathies
I will know you to find you   truth as the only sound

Unburied

should this daze bring
rescue from the other

to drown continents of old lust, to wash
in saltwater of apology—
feeling their pearled bodies shiver,
denouncing their deaths
with desperate light—it still gives thanks,
only slower through pain,

but if hope can be unburied,
hope can be

5

AWOKEN IN A FIELD OF LIGHT

> "I live my life in widening circles
> that reach out across the world.
> I may not complete this last one
> but I give myself to it."
>
> —Rainer Maria Rilke, "1.2" *Book of Hours*
> (t. by Anita Barrows and Joanna Macy)

My Dad Laughs

at the windows

        of my years' passing

                in his strongest belief

    in my happiness

      for our gentlest moments

            to reflect each other

         remembering

he returns shape

        to myself

when apart

      again those hands lift me

           high over his head

They Chirp About Destiny

Wonder how the same thunder returns,
last one awake under my parents' roof.
Long Island hovers
in fantasy; continuous cricket cry,
dark nectar of tedium,
after-roast of outlets
recalling Nintendo nights,
a prayer for dead grandparents, friends
fallen out of confidence, left behind
for the better, for delinquency,
to forsake a fable that owned me.

Maybe tonight, I reclaim the restlessness,
the boy who ran from prayers
to pretend God spoke,
backyard smokes sacred release,
unheard. Only water tower wheezing,
bramble rasping. Strange sad that shaped me
binds to this starry sound,
midnight memories driving parkways,
screamers on stereo; sky tastes Atlantic;
long ways back home, to a timid rapture
of my younger brother snoring

in his bed,
steps away from mine.

In My City

tower cranes snare and sow
as I pass jeering draftsmen
but this jilted strip

between highway tunnels
presence demands upon groves

a cedar's arm in silver sleeves
poises frail
bridged across the sun

to balance its length kindles to ignite
but learn tenderness by its breathing

I might remember every old shame
that once moved me yawns tedious

absent among the spurs
of a brave wisp
loamed of ancient pulp

careful sway
conscience entreats
a tiny glowing tone

when focused widens the sound of listening
in a greener gulf of the deadest forest
I feel around me these city streets unfolding

Man Is the Intelligence of His Soil

I clean out my throat, believe
in the seen
and unseen. Thinking keeps
the charade of breathing
through this terror,
loving everything
and one person.

When reasons turn drivel,
sense is manta,
the sky emptying
into sewer drains. I sow
with no bashful soul.
In whispers,
the bitter sweetens.

Eye threads coiling,
loosened yarn balls,
firedrake fingers, breathing
sweetness, laughing at dirt,
my slow tongue circles, to dowse
in summer wash.
Cinematic.

Hollywood's gray, after all.
Pin this script's pages
to my feet,
ink running, lungs discoursing,
deeming universal past as the ocean,
lifting to wherever hope flows
on golden honey.

Nothing is like love
with anyone and everything.
Cosmic asylum.
Out my bedroom window,
Armageddon, raindrops
crystallin splashing
under the speedlights.

Note on Time

I may not speak enough
of your golden soul.

this heart speeds
city strength to stay
like a memory of home in you.
never play patient,
as dayflower beneath
the street; you fix my eye
to meet the sky: to spread its lens.

before, obsessing over *if*'s,
tasting only with teeth, then
you, my reason to rise,
tomorrow's earliest light;

it is all one moment (I believe it real).
in love with you
like Earth's autumnal tide, as floods
over new cement,
every swash engraving stilled streets;

to capture, in the bright of morning,
braille to my pavement.

Final Friend

Delana, I want
forever to rediscover us.
Are you afraid of the blue?
I can't claim my voice. No scribble vibrates
ancient melody changing tune—
no sensemaking of generations.
I love you in the new jungle, reborn,
again and again. And I don't want us to die.

A blackbird beats on, beats on,
and, over peaks especially
softer winds to revel in.
Delana, your song is gentle
ardency in harmony;
share of stardust, too. Destiny
presses into your skin. *Broken wings*
learn to fly. But rest with me, here.

I designed my malleability. Oceans sleep
in you, a daze away
from the daze, and should all else drift,
you set me free, my only healer,
my final friend.
To chase you; long ago, in another life
a crossroad; words to a song
changed everything.

What if we never know?

Long-Sight

There is a room holding this one, a sketch speaking backward. Every person, every tiny thing, rewinds to sulfur. Pollen blows back to the forest, where trunks dance. This continent begins where the moon rises green as the sea, and wind-tossed reeds breathe the stars.

It is the season of night coming as quick as morning. I come apart in the delicate moments, unwound to Delana's breath and rooms full of the scent of sleep. Even our gentle silences feel slower to me. Their embraces strip me bare.

Tolerance means pacing my heart's perimeter. Care is to barter my loud for quiet. The seeker in me will always loom; be it springtime or autumn's clementine haze. My parents' tender routines and the pain of their parents before, it is all part of me—should it build silences, should it take me across the world.

On lonely nights, you must remember the cry of your hometown's train as it carries a cascade far and away into the past. You must remember the rotten in you before you wish it away. Slow goes the old laughter. Slow goes the echo you owned, that owned you. In the meantime, stay quiet and concentrate on the story before you forget all over again.

Waking often happens long after the eyes have opened.

(And there she is, my name in her hands)

Eyes the Color of Inside the Earth

I receive messages
from branches, spaces light falls
through, moments' delay.
In my dream, you are new
physics. Force come alive, roar
future-past. My body,
vapor dressed for cause,

to steal your fantasy,
to continue the refrain,
to drink highlighted streets,
not silent, not still,
no hands on the wheel, highway
gifting tomorrow's bed.
All I want, promised.

No, I want the promise.
The catch of our eyes, the love
of guaranteeing.
The cherry blossoms
don't heed limp seasons ahead
or bare buds. If time bluffs,
why are we brazen

to believe tomorrow
will keep yesterday alive?
Grinding rears up stardust.
Your eyes, brown and gold
like a movement inside Earth.
Ever, my allegiance,
to prize their wander.

Cave Paint and Storm Songs

My blood, my blood.
Though I system a shrine
to my blood's sadness,
like a secret gift to myself,
I vow to spite my zeal.

///

(*I promise to stay*)

///

Leaves carmine, firebrick, burgundy; branches only where brief sun shines. Acorns gutter with butts and soot. Each morning, darkness' shadow. Before us, long ago, words felt like they could change me, and once spoken into the air, they returned to me weeping like I had abandoned them. I felt sorry for the little things I spoke. *I love you.* And who did I love? What did I pray for when I slept alone? Delana, I reread your letter, soft to your word.

I crossed state lines to reach you, build my home near you. Your hair shorter like the days, we became the night. Timber and precipice air twined tongues, as starlets fell on Connecticut Avenue, everything whispering *And Yet. And Yet. And Yet.* Words made sense to me, articulated benevolence. No mystery unfolding, simply truth. How our years now tangle as map lines do.

///

Not yet tomorrow, the sky collapses
to sleep. Cinder in wind, crunch
in leaves, eyes whorl maple.
The hillside chains far, deepest blue.
We ready our bodies to stay,
the heaviest action.
We, not meteorites
in comfort as we descend, but
universes all our own.
Night doesn't forget our oldest movements.
So fast yet now, still,
orbiting, twin constellations
breathing one another,
asleep to the susurrus of a new fall;
Earth's momentum, swan song.

Evening yellow summons, I sponge. Years seep my pores, the quiet—to know peace without the right words. My prayers snap luscious. Feeling lost in a body, a shape; to say I love you with the right words. I need her to remind. Delana, be the one who never leaves. My verses are yours. At night, call my name if you wake. I will be in your dark brightness, calmness uncovering, promising more than forever. The familiar: heel catching dirt, palm swaddles wind. It all pours, pours to nothing. Delana, you make me forget about death. You eat stars as pears from a tree; I write, manipulative, selfish enough to imagine God's laughter—but to stay where you sleep, to join wake; to linger a mother's son, to carry on a father's wish; to befriend a brother: these honors lend a strength to amend myth.

///

And so, it is
a horrible darkness, sometimes.
And so, it is.

Just outside the door,
a harmonious lament
leaps over the world,
a demented moan
tackling every panel
of every rooftop
in the United States,
the longest kind of moment, in the middle of the night,
keen on halting dreams
and waking children;
a greeting
of an underground beast
invading the surface,
torn beyond the crust
to wail a secret sadness
into heaven.

I don't hold my breath
as I allow it to finish.

To Bring a Pulse (A Cry for Everywhen)

a moment might be parched until
you dive entirely into love, childlike.

its blue shuts, like sky
to baby bird, blue.

framing its little form with it,
flooded by chance of a fall.

love, sky fondly stilling
baby bird to kingdom.

kindly doused in drink,
fixing remnants yet to live.

alive within horizon song,
the rest, chatter by the sun.

silent thrust,
reverberant,

softened beak with love, wings raised
on wind's cradle, rinsed without ransom,

adrift, high
over the Dream.

About the Author

Jonathan Koven grew up on Long Island, NY. He holds a BA in English and Creative Writing from American University, works as a technical writer, and reads chapbooks for *Moonstone Arts*. He lives in Philadelphia with his wife Delana, and their cats Peanut Butter and Keebler. He has both fiction and poetry published by Assure Press, Animal Heart Press, Thirty West Publishing, and more. Read Jonathan's poetry debut *Palm Lines* (2020), available from Toho Publishing. His fiction debut *Below Torrential Hill* (2021) is also available, a winner of the Electric Eclectic Novella Prize.

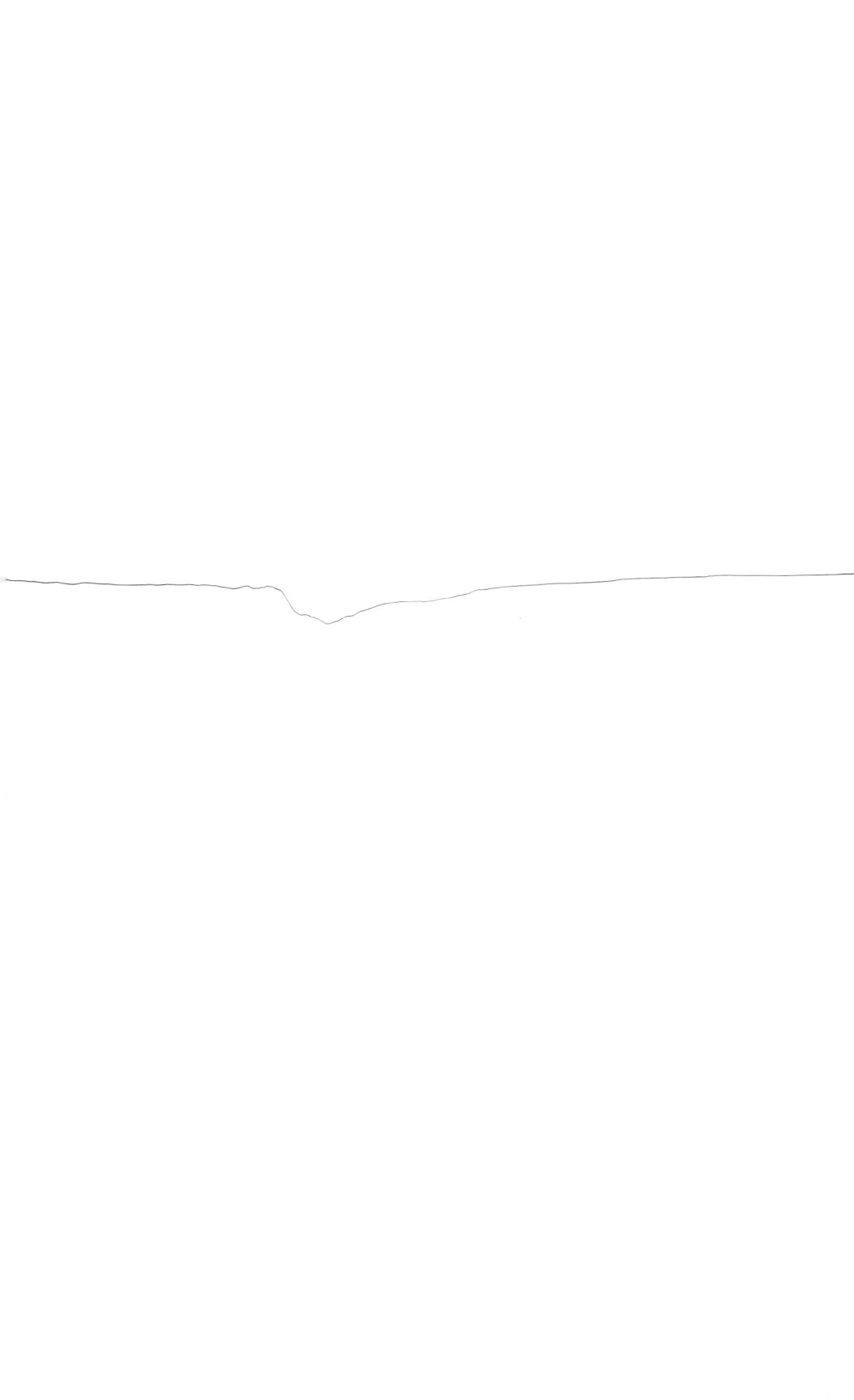

www.ingramcontent.com/pod-product-compliance
Lightning Source LLC
Chambersburg PA
CBHW030909170426
43193CB00009BA/786